A Paper Bag

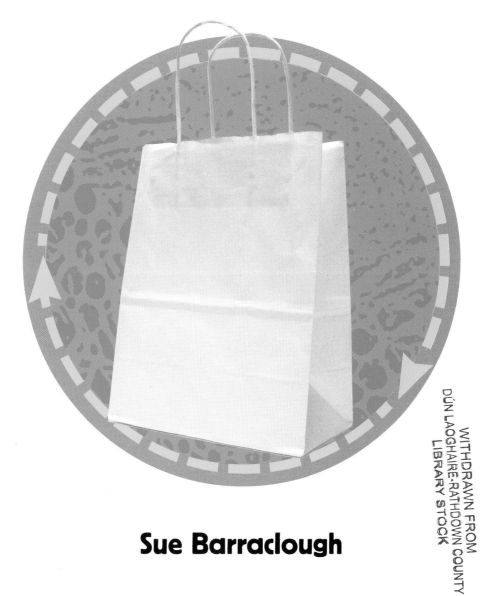

Sue Barraclough

W

FRANKLIN WATTS
LONDON • SYDNEY

First published in 2006 by
Franklin Watts
338 Euston Road
London NW1 3BH

Franklin Watts Australia
Hachette Children's Books
Level 17/207 Kent Street
Sydney NSW 2000

Copyright © Franklin Watts 2006

ISBN: 978 0 7496 6295 0
Dewey classification: 676'.2

Series editor: Sarah Peutrill
Art director: Jonathan Hair
Design: Jemima Lumley
Picture credits: Alamy: front cover tl & b, Back cover tr, 1, 4tl, 27br. Bettmann/Corbis: 23tr. Brand X/Alamy: 22br. Dr. Jeremy Burgess/SPL: 7t. Corbis: 25b. Colin Crisford/Alamy: 22bl. Mark Edwards/Still Pictures: 19b. Werner Forman Archive/Topfoto: 5b. Forest Stewardship Council: 31b. David R. Frazier Photolibrary Inc/Alamy: 17, 26br. Tommaso Guicciardini/SPL: 13t, 26tr. Robert Harding PL: 23bl. Brownie Harris/Corbis: 24t. Jacqui Hurst/Corbis: 14. R. Maisonneuve/Publiphoto Diffusion/SPL: 16tl. Hans Pfetschinger/Still Pictures: 13b. Popperfoto: 9b. Charles O Rear/Corbis: 9tl. Alex Segre/Rex Features: 21, 27bl. Friedrich Stark/Still Pictures: 16br. Stora Enso (Lasse Arvidsson and Birger Roos): front cover cl, c & cr, back cover cl, c, 4tr, 4b, 5t, 6t, 6b, 7b, 8, 9tr, 10tr, 11tl, 11tr, 11b, 12t, 15t, 15b, 16bl, 18t, 18b, 19tr, 20t, 20b, 22t, 26tl, 26cl, 26bl, 26cr, 27tl, 27cl, 30t, 30b, 31c. Kaj R Svensoson/SPL: 12b. Visions of America, LLC/Alamy: 10bl. Every attempt has been made to clear copyright. Should there be any inadvertent omission please apply to the publisher for rectification.

A CIP catalogue record for this book is available from the British Library.

Printed in Malaysia

Franklin Watts is a division of Hachette Children's Books.

Contents

This bag is made from paper.

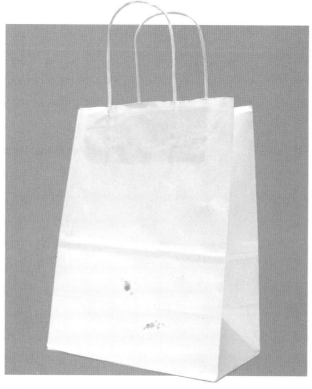

▲ Paper bags like this are made to carry shopping.

The story of a paper bag starts with a living, growing tree. Most paper is made from wood.

▲ Living trees provide wood, which we use to make paper.

What is paper?

Paper is a product that has a wide range of uses. It can be made from the fibres of fabrics, wood or other plant materials. It can be recycled and it is biodegradable, which means that it will rot away.

Can you imagine the process that makes smooth, flexible paper from hard, rough trees?

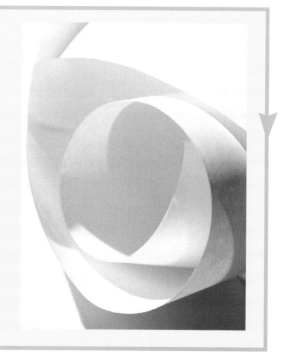

Some types of wood are better for making paper than others. The trees that provide this wood are specially grown on plantations. A plantation is an area of trees planted in tidy rows. Semi-natural forests are also used.

▶ Pine trees can be planted close together because they grow tall and straight.

In the past

The ancient Egyptians made the earliest kind of paper from the papyrus plant. Very thin slices of the plant were glued together to form sheets.

A sheet of Egyptian paper from around 1295-1186 BCE.

Paper formed from fibre pulp may have been first made in China in 105 CE by a man called Ts'ai Lun. He made his paper from the bark of the Mulberry tree, hemp and scraps of linen and cotton. The fibres were mashed and mixed with water. The fibre pulp was pressed into mats, then left to dry in the sun. Paper making spread all over Asia, and finally to Europe in around 1009 CE. The French and Italians then led the paper industry from 1250 to 1470. The first American paper mill opened in Philadelphia in 1690.

Trees are grown to produce wood to make paper.

In tree plantations just one type of tree is grown. This makes the trees easier to look after.

▶ This is a greenhouse where tiny eucalyptus seedlings are grown.

▲ This worker is planting seedlings.

When the trees are harvested or felled, they are replaced with new trees. So plantations have trees at different growth stages. Some trees are ready to be cut down. Other areas are full of small trees. There are also greenhouses with tiny seedlings beginning to grow. These seedlings will be planted in areas where the trees have been harvested.

Some trees, such as eucalyptus trees, grow much faster than others. These trees are most likely to be grown for paper making.

➤ This tiny eucalyptus tree will grow fast, straight and tall. It will take around eight years for this tree to grow big enough to be used in paper making.

▲ You can see the difference between the areas of natural, mixed forest and neatly planted rows of eucalyptus trees in this plantation in Brazil.

In the past
Until the mid-1800s, paper was made from recycled materials such as linen and cotton rags. Paper was made in small amounts and was a lot more rare than it is today.

The trees are cut down and chopped up.

Different trees produce hard and soft wood. The different types of wood make different types of paper. Hardwoods, include the eucalyptus and birch, while softwoods are produced by trees such as pine and spruce.

The trees are cut down and chopped into lengths by a harvester machine. The wood will then be sorted into hardwood and softwood.

▶ This harvester can do several jobs. It cuts the tree down, cuts it into lengths and sorts it into piles.

Then the logs are transported by road, water or rail to the pulp mills.

△ Cranes lift heavy logs onto trucks.

◄ Tugboats move a huge raft of logs across a river.

In the past

In the 1840s when trees became more widely used to make paper, lumber camps sprang up wherever there were large areas of forest. Men flocked to these camps to work as lumberjacks. The lumberjacks chopped down each tree with an axe or a saw.

A lumberjack in the 1950s.

Paper is made from wood fibres.

To make pulp, all the fibres that form the wood need to be broken down and separated. The fibres are put back together in a different way to make the paper.

▶ The fibres in wood make it strong and hard. This wood has to be broken down to make paper.

Each ring shows one year's growth.   Bark (on the outside)

▲ These huge logs need to have their bark removed.

At the pulp mill, the logs are sprayed with water and put into large drums. The drums turn and tumble the logs against each other until they are stripped of their rough outer layer of bark.

Then the logs are fed into a chipper, which cuts them down into small squares called chips.

▼ These wood chips are ready for the next stage.

➤ At a pulp mill, huge mountains of chips are processed day and night.

Why wood?

Wood is widely used for paper making because it is easily available and is best for the job. Different types of wood pulp can be used to produce a range of different papers, from thick card to thin tissue paper. Hardwoods such as birch and eucalyptus have short fibres, which make smooth paper. Softwoods such as pine and spruce have long fibres, which make strong paper. These two are often combined to make strong, smooth paper.

You can see the fibres in this torn paper.

Water, chemicals and heat turn the wood into a pulp.

Wood fibres are held together by a glue-like substance called lignin. The lignin must be removed in order to separate the fibres.

▶ Networks of pipes bring water, chemicals and other ingredients into the pulp-making process.

The wood chips are mixed with water and chemicals, and heated in big metal containers called digesters.

◀ Wood chips are fed into a digester, which separates the fibres.

The heat and chemicals melt the lignin and turn the hard wood chips into a porridge-like pulp.

► The hard wood chips are now a pulpy mush.

In the past

A French scientist called Rene de Reaumur may have had the idea of using wood fibres to make paper, in 1719. He watched a wasp making its nest, and noticed how it turned small pieces of wood into a paper paste.

However, many people think that all the credit goes to the Chinese (see page 5).

These 'paper wasps' use the same basic recipe to make their nests as we do for making paper. They chew small pieces of wood mixed with their saliva. This makes a paste that they mould to make their nests.

The pulp is bleached.

Bleaching makes the pulp white. This is usually done to printing papers. Some pulp is not bleached and it is used to make brown grocery bags and cardboard boxes. Our bag is white so it is made from bleached pulp. Other ingredients can also be added to pulp to make different types of paper. Different ingredients can give the paper texture or colour, or make it stronger. Recycled pulp can also be added.

▽ The paper pulp is brown. This pulp will be bleached white with a gas called oxygen.

The papermaker decides on a mixture of pulps. He or she mixes the pulps to make sure the paper bag has the right strength and will not split easily.

Sheets of paper   Bleached pulp

▶ The pulp goes through many stages to be made into paper. This shows the bleached pulp.

Why recycle paper?

By recycling paper we use fewer trees, less energy and we create less pollution and use less water. Most of the paper we use can be collected and sorted, and turned back into recycled fibre. However, some strong new tree fibre is added to the pulp at the paper mill, because repeated recycling weakens the fibres. So if you want to help to save our forests and be environmentally friendly, recycle all your paper.

Some pulp mills now use recycled paper as their main source of material.

The pulp is checked before being taken to the paper mill.

Quality checking happens at every stage of the process. Samples are taken to make sure the properties of the pulp are right.

▲ A worker takes a sample of pulp.

Now the pulp is ready to go to the paper mill. Here, paper production begins by mixing the pulp with more water to get a slurry. Most of this has to be removed in the paper-making machine.

Traditional methods

Traditional methods of making paper are still used in many parts of the world. This woman is draining water from her paper pulp. The sheet of paper is starting to form in the tray.

The paper-making machine has several sections that remove the water. First, the wet mixture goes into the headbox. This spreads the mixture evenly onto a quickly moving wire mesh tray. Some of the water drops out of the pulp. Next, the pulp is squeezed between rollers. Then the pulp is pressed between materials that soak up even more water.

▼ The wet paper pulp called fibre slurry is spread onto a wire tray.

The paper is pressed and dried.

In the press section, the fibres are pressed tighter and tighter together. This removes more water and increases the strength of the paper. In the drying section the sheets are dried with steam heated cylinders.

Next, the paper is coated with a thin layer of starch in the size press. This coating makes sure that printing inks will not soak into the paper.

The paper is sized (reeled) through the size press.

The paper now goes through the calender section. This is a machine with polished steel rolls. The calender uses heat and pressure to make the paper the same thickness all over. The paper is reeled into jumbo rolls.

▽ The paper is now in a jumbo roll.

Traditional paper drying

Once paper pulp is bonded together to make paper, it needs to be pressed and then dried. In traditional paper-making, the sheets

of paper are hung on a line to dry - just like clothes.

In India handmade paper is produced using traditional methods. Recycled paper pulp is often used.

The jumbo rolls are sliced into smaller rolls.

Sheets of thick paper are wrapped around the small rolls to protect them.

► The smaller rolls can be moved around the mill quickly.

▼ Every stage of the process at the paper mill is carefully checked and controlled.

The paper is ready to be transported to paper merchants and printers. The rolls can be cut down further to make small sheets for writing paper and envelopes. Whole rolls of paper are sent to printers to produce books and newspapers.

Paper is also used for all sorts of packaging, such as boxes, milk cartons, wrappers and bags. The paper for making bags is sent in big batches to the factory.

▶ The heavy rolls of paper are transported in a truck to the paper bag manufacturer.

Why paper?

Around half of all the paper produced worldwide is used in packaging. Paper is popular for packaging because it can be made into many different types. It can be soft, strong, lightweight, waterproof or textured. It is also flexible so it can be folded and moulded into different shapes. Recycled paper is often also used for packaging papers. The other advantage is, unlike plastic, which is also popular for packaging, paper will rot if it is thrown away.

The paper bag is designed.

▲ Virtual packaging technology means designs can be tried and tested on screen.

To produce a paper shopping bag, the designer chooses the paper and colours. The design of the bag needs to suit its purpose. The designer decides how the handles, if there are any, will be added, and what material will be used to make them.

In the past

Early shopkeepers would simply wrap shopping in paper, or maybe twist some paper into a cone to hold something. Today, we have a huge variety of different bags, from simple brown paper bags to smart, brightly-printed shopping bags.

This bag is a simple cylinder of paper, glued at one end.

Margaret Knight (1838-1914) invented a part for a machine to make a square-bottomed bag.

▲ All these paper bags have different designs. Look at the shapes and sizes, and the different handles.

▲ Printing is an important part of some bags. Logos or patterns advertise certain shops or products.

Paper and printing

Gutenberg (right) in his workshop.

The invention of the moveable type printing press, by German inventor Johannes Gutenberg in 1453, was a turning point for paper making. Books could be made more cheaply and quickly, so they became more widely available. As printing technology changed, the demand for paper grew. There were not enough rags, still the main source of fibre, to make so much paper. Other materials such as straw and hemp depended on seasonal harvests. So papermakers needed to find another source of fibre. However, it wasn't until the mid-1800s that wood pulp became widely used.

A machine makes the paper bags.

Once the design is finished, the paper bag is made by a machine. Bags can be made faster, cheaper and neater by a machine than if they were made by hand.

▲ The paper is cut into sheets of the right size.

Sheets of paper are fed into one end of the paper bag machine and the finished bags come out at the other end.

◀ As the paper goes through the machine, it is creased and folded.

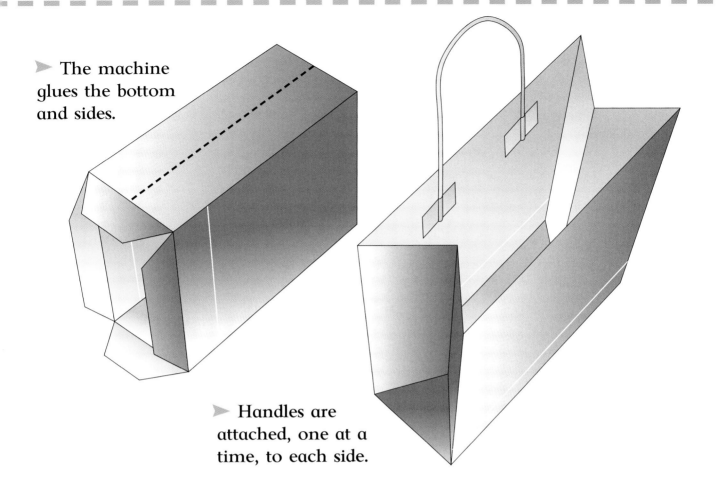

➤ The machine glues the bottom and sides.

➤ Handles are attached, one at a time, to each side.

The bags can be folded flat and packed up. Then they are sent out to shops ready to be used to carry your shopping.

◀ Do you prefer paper or plastic bags to carry your shopping?

How a paper bag is made

1. Trees are grown in plantations or they grow in semi-natural forests.

4. Water and heat turn the wood chips into a mushy pulp.

2. The trees are cut down, sorted and transported. New trees are planted in their place.

5. The pulp is bleached.

3. The wood is chopped into small chips.

6. Water is added to the pulp. The wet slurry is spread on a wire tray to drain it and the drying process begins.

7. The pulp is run through rollers. The fibres are pressed and stretched into sheets as they are dried.

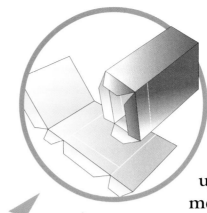

10. The paper is cut down and the paper bag is made up in a machine.

11. The paper bag is ready to use. After it has been used, it can be recycled.

8. The calender uses heat and pressure to make the paper the same thickness all over. Then the paper is reeled into jumbo rolls.

9. The jumbo roll is cut down into smaller rolls and they are taken to the bag manufacturer.

Paper and its many uses

It is hard to imagine a world without paper. Think of all the everyday items we use, such as books, magazines, birthday cards, leaflets and posters. From tissues and toilet paper to cereal boxes and milk cartons, paper is everywhere in our homes.

➤ Paper can be dyed with bright colours. This paper is smooth which makes it an ideal surface for writing or drawing.

▼ Paper is light and is easy to bend and crease, so it makes perfect fans.

▲ Paper can be used to make cartons like these.

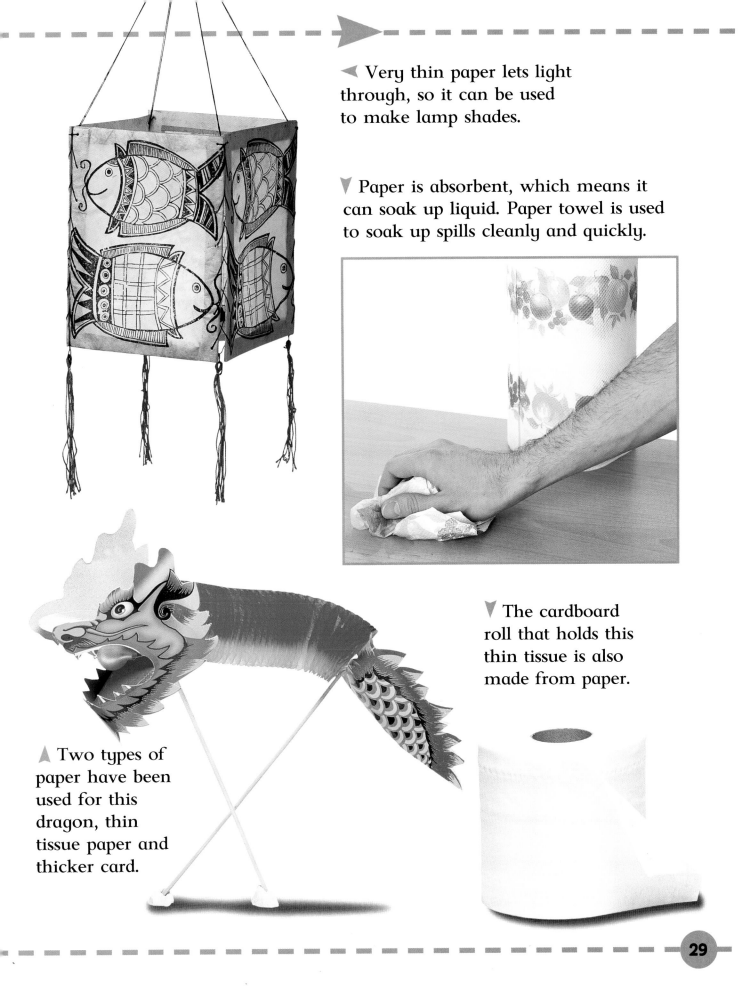

◀ Very thin paper lets light through, so it can be used to make lamp shades.

▼ Paper is absorbent, which means it can soak up liquid. Paper towel is used to soak up spills cleanly and quickly.

▼ The cardboard roll that holds this thin tissue is also made from paper.

▲ Two types of paper have been used for this dragon, thin tissue paper and thicker card.

Paper and the environment

Trees are an important resource, which we can all help to protect.

Reducing waste

Paper and wood companies do not waste any part of a tree that is cut down.

Managing forests

Many paper companies manage forests responsibly. They plant a seedling for each tree they cut down or leave seeds dropped by trees to grow naturally.

The smallest pieces of wood are used as biofuel.

Small trunk parts are used to make paper and chipboard.

Thicker parts of the trunk are used for timber and paper making.

Sawmill leftovers are used to make paper and chipboard.

◄ Around 30% of the wood can be used for sawn products, 70% for pulp and paper.

Many places have recycling collection schemes.

We can help

Paper was once rare, but now it is made on a huge scale, and it is cheap and widely available. The best way we can help is to use less paper and recycle what we do use.

Protecting natural forests

The FSC is the Forest Stewardship Council. It was set up to conserve the world's forests. Forests are vital for the well-being of the Earth, but much of our natural forests have already been destroyed. The FSC makes sure that our remaining natural forests are left untouched, and that plantations that produce wood are also managed well.

If you see this sign on wood, you know it has been taken from well-managed forests.

The other major forest certification schemes in Europe and North America are:
The Programme for the Endorsement of Forest Certification Schemes
The Sustainable Forest Initiative
Canadian Standards Association

Around the world there are many more schemes. About 5% of global forests have been certified. In Western Europe and North America this is much higher at 30-50%. Find out more at:
www.fsc.org
www.pefc.org
www.aboutsfi.org
www.sfms.com

Word bank

Biodegradable Any material that can be broken down naturally in the environment.

Biofuel Fuel made from renewable raw materials such as bark and logging leftovers.

Calendering The process of reeling paper round steel rolls to make the paper the same thickness all over.

Chemical A substance made up of atoms. Atoms are the building blocks that make up different substances.

Chipboard A thin board made of wood chips that are pressed and glued together.

Digesters These containers are used to heat and soften the wood chips. This melts the lignin, a natural glue, which holds the wood fibres together.

Headbox The headbox is a part at the start of a paper-making machine. It is a huge nozzle that spreads the paper pulp evenly onto a wire tray.

Oxygen A gas found in air and water. The air that we breathe is a mixture of oxygen and other gases. The green parts of plants produce oxygen.

Pollution When air, water or land are made dirty or poisoned by harmful substances.

Process A series of actions that produce a change.

Recycled A material that has been processed so that it can be re-used.

Semi-natural forest A forest that has grown naturally but is now partly managed by a business who plant and harvest trees.

Index